Kids in the Holiday Kitchen

Making Baking Giving

By Jessica Strand & Tammy Massman-Johnson
Photographs by James Baigrie

CHRONICLE BOOKS
SAN FRANCISCO

Library of Congress Cataloging-in-Publication Data
available.

ISBN-10: 0-8118-6139-2
ISBN-13: 978-0-8118-6139-7

Manufactured in China.

Designed by Domino Design
Prop styling by Lynda White
Food styling by Sara Neumeier
Assistant photography by Gayle Brooker
Assistant prop styling by Jeff Wood

Distributed in Canada by Raincoast Books
9050 Shaughnessy Street
Vancouver, British Columbia V6P 6E5

10 9 8 7 6 5 4 3 2 1

Chronicle Books LLC
680 Second Street
San Francisco, California 94107

www.chroniclebooks.com

The publisher wishes to thank Williams-Sonoma for
providing serving ware, utensils, and accoutrements used
in many of the photos in this book.

Cuisinart is a registered trademark of Conair Corporation,
Hershey's Kisses is a registered trademark of Hershey
Chocolate & Confectionery Corporation, Life Savers is a
registered trademark of Nabisco Brands Co., Necco is
a registered trademark of New England Confectionery Co.,
Oreo is a registered trademark of Kraft Foods Holdings,
Inc., Original Heath is a registered trademark of Leaf, Inc.,
Popsicle is a registered trademark of Good Humor-Breyers,
Red Hot is a registered trademark of Ferrara Pan Candy
Co., Inc., Reese's is a registered trademark of Hershey
Chocolate & Confectionery Corporation, Tupperware is a
registered trademark of Dart Industries, Williams-Sonoma is
a registered trademark of Williams-Sonoma, Inc., Ziploc is a
registered trademark of S.C. Johnson Home Storage, Inc.

TO STEPHEN AND LUCIAN, WHO MAKE ALL MY HOLIDAYS WARM AND WONDERFUL.

What would we be without the help, guidance, and support of a team of exceptional editors—thank you Leslie Jonath, Amy Treadwell, and Jan Hughes. Where would this book be without the keen vision, brilliance, and patience of Laurel Leigh, who time and time again manages this and other projects of mine with great enthusiasm and expertise. This book would not look as lovely and adorable as it does without Pamela Geismar's exceptional design and James Baigrie's lovely photographs. Thank you! We also have to thank again and again the other significant players, Ann Rolke, Mike Ashby, Carrie Bradley, and Jane Chinn, who worked tirelessly to make sure this book was as pristine and perfect as it can be, and delightful models, Samantha Armengau, Gorge Ostolaza, and Asa Friedrich, who graced the pages with cheerful smiles. I also would like to thank my partner Tammy, who made this book a delight, a breeze, and just plain fun to create. Thank you for all your creative genius, patience, and hard work! —Jessica

**TO LUKE, FOR BEING ALL THE BEST INGREDIENTS,
AND TO ZOË AND MIKAH, MY MOST DELICIOUS LITTLE MORSELS.**

A huge thank you to Jessica, for inviting me into the Holiday Kitchen, for her invaluable guidance, humor, and, mostly, for her warm and wonderful partnership and friendship. Thank you also to my husband, Luke, for his unwavering patience (always!), computer expertise, and tireless enthusiasm and support. He is my much better half and my hero. And to Zoë and Mikah, whose little cooking and crafting hands are huge inspiration for me. Thank you for being you. —Tammy

CONTENTS

Sweet Somethings

Happy Holiday Workshop

READY, SET, FUN
Introduction

Welcome to *Kids in the Holiday Kitchen*, our all-inclusive answer to a creative, stress-free celebratory season. It is a well-known fact that between shopping, cooking, tree trimming, gift-wrapping, and entertaining, the magic of the holidays often turns to mayhem!

As two mothers ourselves, we realize the need for a book that combines holiday cooking, baking, crafting, and even homemade gifts into an organized how-to guide. In the spirit of artistic, culinary, and creative adventure, we've written *Kids in the Holiday Kitchen* as a way for kids and adults to participate together in the joys of the holiday season.

You'll find Tips and Tools and How to Be Careful in the beginning of this book, which serves as a guide to what you need, what might be helpful, and how to be aware and cautious while working on these crafts, confections, and dishes. It's best to go over these pages with your kids before delving into the recipes and projects.

The book is divided into four fun chapters: **MEALTIME MAGIC**, **NAUGHTY AND NICE NIBBLES**, **SWEET SOMETHINGS**, and **HAPPY HOLIDAY WORKSHOP**. Each section focuses on a different kind of cooking or crafting activity that you can do with kids ages four and up. By reading the instructions, you can decide which steps would feel most appropriate for your child to do in the kitchen. Of course, you can mix and match recipes in each section; please do not feel restricted by the chapter titles.

MEALTIME MAGIC offers an array of tasty recipes to sate your kids' holiday appetites. We can't think of dishes that are more comforting than creamy cups of tomato soup and crispy, melted grilled cheese sandwiches, or individual ramekins filled to the brim with gooey, rich macaroni crowned by golden crusts.

As for **NAUGHTY AND NICE NIBBLES**, need we say more? This section was conceived with noshing in mind. Whether the snacks are healthy like Blixen's Mix, filled with nuts and dried fruits, or decadent like New Year's Nuggets, a crunchy caramel corn drizzled with smooth milk chocolate, the nibbles are sublime. Kids and parents alike (and uncles, aunts, grandmas, grandpas, and older siblings) will enjoy dipping their spoons, forks, and occasionally their hands into these delicious kitchen creations.

Of course, you can't have a holiday book without offering a chapter completely devoted to serious treats. **SWEET SOMETHINGS** range from classic homemade ice cream sandwiches in the shape of Christmas trees to the ultimate oatmeal cookie crammed with chewy cherries, crunchy coconut, and dark chocolate chips. Remember, this time of year is supposed to be sweet!

The **HAPPY HOLIDAY WORKSHOP** is filled with wonderful gift and holiday decoration ideas, from homemade greeting cards like Happy Hellos to Sweet and Crunchy Garland—an edible extravaganza of popcorn, gumdrops, and candies. You may want to gather a group of your kids' friends and have a holiday bash where you pick two or three crafts for them to make. At the party you can offer Sleigh Rider Cider (page 39), Skater's Dip (page 32), and an assortment of North Pole Delights (page 61) and Reindeer Bark (page 33) for them to snack on. We know, having had these gatherings at our own homes, that children leave the party thrilled to have made their very own holiday creations.

Between kids, grown-ups, tweens, and teens, there are recipes and projects galore, so go ahead and cook, craft, create, and explore. Most of all, have fun! The dishes are absolutely delicious, the sweets scrumptious, and the inventive crafts will be treasured for years to come.

With this book, we wish you an inspired holiday and a happy new year. Welcome to the Holiday Kitchen … enjoy!

—Jessica & Tammy & our helpers: Lucian, age 7; Zoë, age 6; Mikah, age 4

TIPS AND TOOLS
Ingredients and Utensils

TIPS

Some recipes and crafts in this book are geared for younger children, while some are more appropriate for older kids. Before making a craft or recipe, decide if it is appropriate for your child's age group.

The crafts in this book are intended to take an hour or less to make; some (like Happy Hellos and Jingling Jewel Balls) require only 10 to 15 minutes. If you host a holiday craft party, plan accordingly.

Look at the time the recipe takes, and be sure you have time to complete the project and clean up. It's important not to rush through any of these crafts or recipes because that's when most accidents happen.

Look at the instructions. Do things need to be chopped or sliced, cut or diced before you begin the recipe? If they do, make sure to get all the ingredients or items ready to be crafted or cooked.

Organize yourself completely. Make sure to have available all the ingredients and tools you need.

Before you begin cooking or doing a craft, make sure to read the directions very carefully.

Try to create a relaxed, calm environment. If a spill occurs … it's just a spill. These crafts and recipes are meant to be entertaining, not anxiety provoking.

And, always remember the most important and basic recipe: kids + adults + making stuff together = fun fun fun!

TOOLS

Many of the tools you will need to complete the projects in this book are standard kitchen or household items, but a few you may need to buy. Make a game out of listing, finding, and going on a shopping adventure to purchase the necessary tools and ingredients for the recipes and crafts your group selects. Carry this book with you, or make a copy of the pages needed, and let kids keep track as each new treasure is added to the shopping cart.

Aluminum foil
Aprons (optional)
Baking dishes
Blender or Cuisinart
Box grater/shredder
Cookie cutters
Cooling (wire) racks
Electric mixer
Fine-mesh sieve
Forks
Hot-glue gun
Icing spatula
Juicer (optional)
Knives
Measuring cups
Measuring spoons
Mini loaf pan
Mixing bowls

Muffin pans
Newspaper (to cover work surfaces)
Paper towels
Parchment paper
Plastic wrap
Potholders
Rags (optional, for cleanup)
Rolling pin
Rubber spatula
Saucepans (large, medium, and small)
Spoons
Stockpot
Wire cutter
Wooden mixing spoons
Zester (optional)

HOW TO BE CAREFUL
Safety Guidelines

☞ Adult supervision is necessary for the cooking and craft recipes in this book.

☞ Remember to always wash your hands before you start a recipe.

☞ Knives and tools can be sharp. Use caution.

☞ Young children need adult assistance in crafts requiring a hot-glue gun, needles, wire, and wire cutters.

☞ Working around a hot stove or oven can be very dangerous. Always use dry oven mitts when handling pans or cookie sheets.

☞ Keep long hair tied back while cooking.

☞ Wear clothes that you don't mind getting dirty or staining, or wear an apron.

☞ Create a designated work space to do your crafts or cooking. Use one area for crafts, and a separate area for cooking.

☞ Don't wash a hot pan. Let it cool before you put it in the sink.

☞ Clean up after yourself as you are working on your projects. Messy spaces can become dangerous.

☞ Don't crowd the kitchen or craft area. Kids can get burned or hurt if there are too many people in a small space. Always be careful when handling hot pans, pots, or dishes.

☞ Be careful when using any electric tools (like a mixer). Your hands should be dry before you use tools, and make sure to unplug them when you're finished.

☞ Never walk around the kitchen carrying a knife. Have an adult deal with any sharp knives.

MEALTIME MAGIC

These yummy breakfast, lunch, and dinner dishes are made with kids in mind. They'll love to create food for the whole family. We've included our old favorites, as well as recent winners to inspire each and every one in your house to get cooking.

HAPPY HOLIDAY PUFF
Breakfast Cheese Soufflé

This fun twist on a classic recipe comes from Tammy's mom, who has been making her famous soufflé for holiday get-togethers for the last thirty years. She serves it piping hot, alongside latkes (page 25) and a platter of bagels, lox, and cream cheese. A big bowl of fresh berries perfectly rounds off this feast. Needless to say, everyone loosens their belt a notch (or two!) before leaving the table. It tastes best when prepared the night before and baked the next morning.

6 large eggs, separated

1 cup whole milk

1 (12-ounce) can evaporated milk

Pinch dry mustard

Pinch ground allspice

Pinch salt

1 (1½-pound) loaf sliced egg bread, crusts removed, each slice quartered

4 ounces (1 stick) unsalted butter, melted, plus extra for greasing the dish

2 cups freshly shredded Swiss cheese

¼ cup dried onion flakes

2 cups freshly shredded Cheddar cheese

☃ **Grease** a 9 x 13-inch baking dish.

☃ **In a large bowl,** whisk together the egg yolks, whole milk, evaporated milk, dry mustard, allspice, and salt. Set aside.

☃ **Cover the bottom of the baking dish** with 1 layer of bread slices. Using a pastry brush, lightly brush this bread layer with ¼ cup of the melted butter. Sprinkle the Swiss cheese evenly on top and then sprinkle 2 tablespoons of the onion flakes on top of the cheese.

☃ **Repeat this process** with a second layer of bread, remaining ¼ cup melted butter, Cheddar cheese, and remaining 2 tablespoons onion flakes.

☃ **In a mixer,** beat the egg whites until soft peaks form; fold the whites into the yolk mixture and gently combine. Pour this mixture over the bread and cheese; smooth the top with a spatula.

☃ **Cover with foil** and refrigerate overnight.

☃ **Preheat the oven** to 325 degrees F.

☃ **Bake** until the soufflé is risen and golden, 35 to 45 minutes. Serve immediately.

SERVES 8

TOAST TIME
Stuffed French Toast

A twist on the traditional fried Hanukkah doughnuts, this stuffed and sautéed French toast is much healthier, and far more delicious! Tammy's mother-in-law, Dana, has eleven grandchildren, who line up for this dish every year, and lucky for them, she has never disappointed. Most of the kids are finally old enough to help with the cooking, and every one of them is able to "clean" their plate, so to speak!

8 ounces cream cheese, at room temperature

2 teaspoons vanilla extract, divided

½ cup chopped walnuts

1 (1½-pound) loaf French bread

4 large eggs

1 teaspoon ground nutmeg

1 cup heavy whipping cream

SYRUP

1 (12-ounce) jar apricot preserves

½ cup orange juice

2 tablespoons honey

In a mixer, beat the cream cheese with 1 teaspoon of the vanilla until smooth. Stir in the nuts.

Cut the French bread into twelve 1½-inch slices. Cut a pocket in the side of each slice, and fill it with some of the cream cheese–nut mix.

Beat together the eggs, remaining 1 teaspoon vanilla, the nutmeg, and the whipping cream. Dip the bread into this mixture. Cook on a lightly greased griddle until golden, 2 to 3 minutes per side. Keep the toast warm in the oven while making the syrup.

To make the syrup: In a saucepan, stir together the apricot preserves, orange juice, and honey over medium-low heat until hot. Serve with the warm French toast.

SERVES 6

TEACUP SOUP AND SNOWMAN SANDWICHES
Tomato Soup and Grilled Cheese Sandwiches

Here's a little comfort food to warm your tummy. Feel free to use mugs or fun teacups, and use any semi-large cookie cutter your heart desires when it comes to making your special holiday grilled cheese.

TOMATO SOUP

¼ cup olive oil

1 large onion, coarsely chopped

1 tablespoon minced garlic

2 (14-ounce) cans whole peeled Italian tomatoes with juice

2½ cups chicken stock

3 tablespoons tomato paste

⅛ teaspoon ground nutmeg

1 cup whole milk

Sea salt and freshly cracked black pepper

GRILLED CHEESE SANDWICHES

12 slices Cheddar, Muenster, or Havarti cheese

12 slices whole wheat bread

6 ounces (1½ sticks) unsalted butter

To make the soup: In a large stockpot, heat the olive oil over medium heat. Add the onion and sauté until translucent, 3 to 5 minutes. Add the garlic, and sauté for about 1 minute.

Add the tomatoes, stock, tomato paste, and nutmeg. Bring to a boil, reduce the heat, and allow it to simmer uncovered until the flavors meld together, 30 to 40 minutes.

Working in batches, place the soup into a blender, and puree. Pour the pureed soup back into the stockpot, and add the milk. Bring it to a simmer over low heat. Season with salt and pepper to taste. Pour into 6 decorative teacups, and serve. If made ahead, reheat in a large pot over medium heat, stirring for 5 minutes, or until hot.

To make the sandwiches: Place 2 slices of cheese between 2 slices of wheat bread. In a large skillet or on a stove-top grill, melt 2 to 3 tablespoons of butter, then place 2 to 3 sandwiches in the skillet (making sure that they are sitting flat and are not crowded).

Press the sandwiches down with a spatula. When the sandwiches are golden on the bottom, flip onto the other side. Add 2 to 3 tablespoons more butter, making sure to keep the surface well greased. When golden on both sides, transfer to a cutting surface. Repeat to make the remaining sandwiches.

Press a large snowman or other cookie cutter into the center of each sandwich. Remove the remnants. Place your ornamental sandwiches on a plate, and serve with the tomato soup.

SERVES 6

RUDOLPH'S RED SAUCE PASTA
Homemade Marinara with Fusilli

There are some cases where messing with a classic makes complete sense, but when it comes to your basic pasta and red sauce, why bother? It's a taste that has warmed the hearts and bellies of millions of kids for years over. Here's our version, which is just as much a crowd-pleaser with the kids as it is with Grandma and Grandpa.

3 tablespoons extra-virgin olive oil

1 clove garlic, minced

1 small yellow onion, coarsely chopped

4 cups peeled and chopped Italian tomatoes or canned tomatoes

1 tablespoon balsamic vinegar

Salt and freshly ground black pepper

1½ pounds dried fusilli pasta

¾ cup finely grated fresh Parmesan cheese (optional)

❊ **In a large saucepan,** heat the olive oil over medium heat. Add the garlic and onion and sauté for 3 minutes. Add the tomatoes and stir. Let the tomatoes simmer for 5 minutes, then add the vinegar and salt and pepper to taste. Turn the heat down to low.

❊ **Fill a large stockpot** ½ to ¾ full of water. When the water boils, add a pinch of salt and the pasta. Cook until al dente (tender but firm to the bite).

❊ **Drain the pasta.** Add the pasta to the sauce and toss. Sprinkle with the Parmesan, if desired, and serve immediately.

SERVES 6

KRISS KRINGLES
Chicken Fritters with Honey-Mustard Dipping Sauce

This mock fried chicken is a fun food to make with a bunch of kids. Everyone can throw an ingredient into the brown bag and everyone gets a chance to shake and coat the chicken fritters. As for the cooking, that's for the older folks in the house. You can certainly serve the fritters on individual plates, but we like to make it a hearty nosh by presenting it on a big platter with the dipping sauce in the center.

HONEY-MUSTARD DIPPING SAUCE

½ cup mayonnaise

3 tablespoons honey

2 tablespoons yellow mustard

¼ teaspoon Dijon mustard

1 or 2 tablespoons orange juice

CHICKEN FRITTERS

¾ cup all-purpose flour

¾ cup dried bread crumbs

1 teaspoon paprika

1 teaspoon salt

¾ teaspoon ground nutmeg

½ teaspoon garlic powder

2 large split chicken breasts (about 48 ounces), skinless and boneless, cut into 1 x 3-inch strips

4 tablespoons canola oil

To make the sauce: Whisk together the mayonnaise, honey, and mustards; add orange juice to taste. Set aside while you prepare the chicken.

To make the fritters: In a large brown paper bag, combine the flour, bread crumbs, paprika, salt, nutmeg, and garlic powder. Shake the bag several times. Add 3 to 4 strips of chicken at a time and shake to coat.

Place the floured chicken on a platter.

In a large sauté pan, heat the oil for 2 to 3 minutes. Add some of the chicken fritters, making sure that they are spaced so that all sides fry. Turn the fritters several times, cooking them until golden, 10 to 12 minutes. Remove to paper towels to cool. Repeat with the remaining chicken.

Place the fritters on a large platter with the dipping sauce in the middle and serve.

SERVES 6

LONG LIFE NOODLES
Sesame Noodles with Shredded Cucumber

Your whole family will love these peanut noodles. The intense peanut flavor and the added crunch of cucumber and chopped peanuts makes them utterly sublime. Whether it's the middle of winter or a hot summer day, these noodles are ideal for lunch or dinner.

1 pound dried soba noodles

1½ cucumbers (about 16 ounces), peeled, halved, and seeded

1 cup salted peanut butter

½ cup rice vinegar

6 tablespoons sesame oil

8 tablespoons canola oil, divided

6 tablespoons water

2 cloves garlic, minced

¼ cup coarsely chopped roasted, salted peanuts (optional)

Fill a large stockpot ½ to ¾ full of water. Bring to a boil and cook the noodles until al dente (tender but firm to the bite).

In a food processor fitted with a shredding blade, feed the cucumber through the chute. Once the cucumber is shredded, place it in a large bowl and set aside.

In a food processor fitted with a metal blade or in a blender, combine the peanut butter, vinegar, sesame oil, 6 tablespoons of the canola oil, the water, and garlic. Blend the mixture until smooth.

Drain the noodles and toss with the remaining 2 tablespoons canola oil, then toss with the peanut butter sauce. Let cool. When the noodles are at room temperature, toss in the shredded cucumber. If the noodles seem too dense, add a sprinkling of rice vinegar and water. Garnish with the chopped peanuts, if desired, and serve.

SERVES 6

MERRY MACARONI
Macaroni and Cheese

Creamy, gooey, cheesy, and perfectly golden on top. That's what you're looking for. Keep this recipe handy because this is destined to become a family favorite! We like to use Gruyère cheese, but if you prefer sharp Cheddar or Jack cheese, use them instead.

1 pound dried elbow macaroni

2½ ounces (½ stick plus 1 tablespoon) butter, divided

3 cups grated Gruyère cheese

2½ cups grated Parmesan cheese, divided

½ cup heavy cream

1 cup whole milk

1 teaspoon dry mustard

¼ teaspoon ground nutmeg

Sea salt and freshly cracked black pepper

1 cup fresh bread crumbs

Preheat the oven to 375 degrees F.

In a large pot, cook the macaroni in salted boiling water until al dente (tender but firm to the bite). Drain, and set aside.

Lightly grease 8 (8-ounce) ramekins with 1 table-spoon of the butter.

In a large bowl, whisk together the Gruyère, 2 cups of the Parmesan, the cream, milk, dry mustard, and nutmeg. Add the macaroni and toss until thoroughly coated with the cheese mixture. Add salt and pepper to taste. Transfer to the greased ramekins.

In a small bowl, toss together the bread crumbs and the remaining ½ cup Parmesan. Sprinkle the ramekins evenly with the cheese bread crumbs, and dot each ramekin with ½ tablespoon of the remaining butter.

Bake until the tops are golden, 20 to 25 minutes.

SERVES 8

ALL WRAPPED UP
Smoked Turkey Roll-Ups with Cream Cheese and Cucumber

This healthy snack is quick and fun to make. Put out the ingredients and let the kids go to town. If you want to add mustard or cheese, feel free. We've always thought that the more in a roll-up, the better. Here's a tasty basic recipe that you can add to.

1 pound sliced smoked turkey (18 to 20 slices)

8 ounces whipped cream cheese

2 medium cucumbers, peeled and halved, cut into ½ x 4-inch slivers

On a flat cutting surface, place a slice of turkey, spread it with a thin layer of cream cheese, then lay a cucumber spear lengthwise at 1 end of the turkey. Carefully roll the turkey-cucumber spear up. Repeat with the remaining ingredients.

Place the roll-ups on a platter, and serve.

SERVES 6

LOTS OF LATKES
Potato Pancakes

The smell of these latkes cooking will have friends and family running to the kitchen, and the taste will have them begging for more! Sour cream and homemade applesauce truly bring these symbolic potato treats to life.

HOMEMADE APPLESAUCE

10 sweet unpeeled apples (such as McIntosh, Braeburn, or Fuji), cut into 1-inch cubes

½ cup water

¼ cup sugar

2 teaspoons ground cinnamon

LATKES

8 medium russet potatoes, peeled

2 medium onions, quartered lengthwise, thinly sliced

4 large eggs

1 cup matzo meal

1 tablespoon kosher salt

1 teaspoon freshly ground black pepper

Vegetable oil, for frying

2 cups sour cream

☃ **To make the applesauce:** In a large stockpot, combine all the ingredients and heat over medium-low heat, stirring frequently until soft, about 20 minutes.

☃ **When the apples are tender,** turn off the heat, and gently mash them with a wooden spoon to the desired consistency. This applesauce is delicious warm or cold.

☃ **To make the latkes:** Grate the potatoes and place them in a large bowl. Add the onions and toss together.

☃ **Take a large handful** of potato-onion mixture and squeeze to remove excess water. Pile the mixture onto paper towels. Repeat with the rest of the mixture, changing paper towels if needed. Return the mixture to the dry bowl.

☃ **In a separate bowl,** lightly beat the eggs. Pour the eggs into the potato-onion mixture, and stir, gradually adding the matzo meal. Add the salt and pepper.

☃ **Pour ¾ inch of oil** into a 10- to 12-inch frying pan with sides at least 2 inches high, and heat over medium-high heat for 3 to 4 minutes. Form the batter into thin, palm-sized patties, and carefully place them in the frying pan, 4 patties at a time. Flip your latkes when the bottoms are golden brown. This usually takes 3 to 4 minutes.

☃ **When the latkes are browned** on both sides, place them on paper towels to absorb excess oil, and continue this process with the remaining batter.

☃ **Serve hot,** with sour cream and applesauce.

MAKES 20 LATKES

❄ SNOWBALLS IN THE FOREST
Individual Pesto and Mozzarella Pizzas

Aren't we all tired of the classic cheese and tomato pizza? How about trying a savory, gooey pesto pizza instead? Make sure to get fresh mozzarella—it makes all the difference in creating a cleaner, less oily flavor.

DOUGH

1 packet (2¼ teaspoons) active dry yeast

1½ cups very warm water

2 teaspoons honey

2½ cups whole wheat flour, plus more for dusting

1 tablespoon plus 1 teaspoon olive oil

PESTO

2 cloves garlic

3 cups loosely packed fresh basil

1 cup coarsely grated Parmesan cheese

¼ cup walnuts

¼ cup pine nuts

⅔ cup extra-virgin olive oil

Salt and freshly cracked black pepper

8 ounces fresh mozzarella, cut into ½-inch cubes

❄ **To make the dough:** In a large bowl, add the yeast to the warm water, then stir in the honey. Let it stand until frothy, 10 to 12 minutes. Add the flour and work the mixture into a dough. Add 1 tablespoon of the oil. On a lightly floured surface, knead the dough with your hands, carefully stretching it this way and that until it is smooth. Form into a ball.

❄ **Use the remaining 1 teaspoon oil** to grease a large, clean bowl. Place the dough into the oiled bowl. Cover the bowl with a damp dish towel. Let the dough rise in a warm place until doubled, about 45 minutes.

❄ **Line 2 baking sheets** with foil. Preheat the oven to 425 degrees F.

❄ **Flour a work surface** and your hands and separate the dough into 6 equal balls. Take a ball and use the palm of your hand to push the dough away from you, continuing around and around in a circle until you have a flattened circular crust about 6 inches in diameter. The crust should feel smooth. Repeat with the other dough balls and transfer the crusts to the baking sheets. Cover, and put in a warm place. Make the pesto while the dough is doubling.

✳ **To make the pesto:** In a food processor, chop the garlic until it is completely minced. Add the basil, Parmesan, and nuts, and pulse to blend. With the motor running, slowly add the olive oil through the feed tube in a continuous stream. Keep the motor running until the pesto is fully blended. Add salt and pepper to taste.

✳ **When the crusts have risen,** spread each one with a layer of pesto, and then scatter them with pieces of mozzarella. The cheesier, the better.

✳ **Bake the pizzas** until the cheese is a golden brown, about 20 minutes. Serve immediately.

SERVES 6

NAUGHTY AND NICE NIBBLES

Whether you're naughty or nice,
there's always a nibble. We've included
sweet and savory snacks ... some healthy,
some sinful (but always delicious).

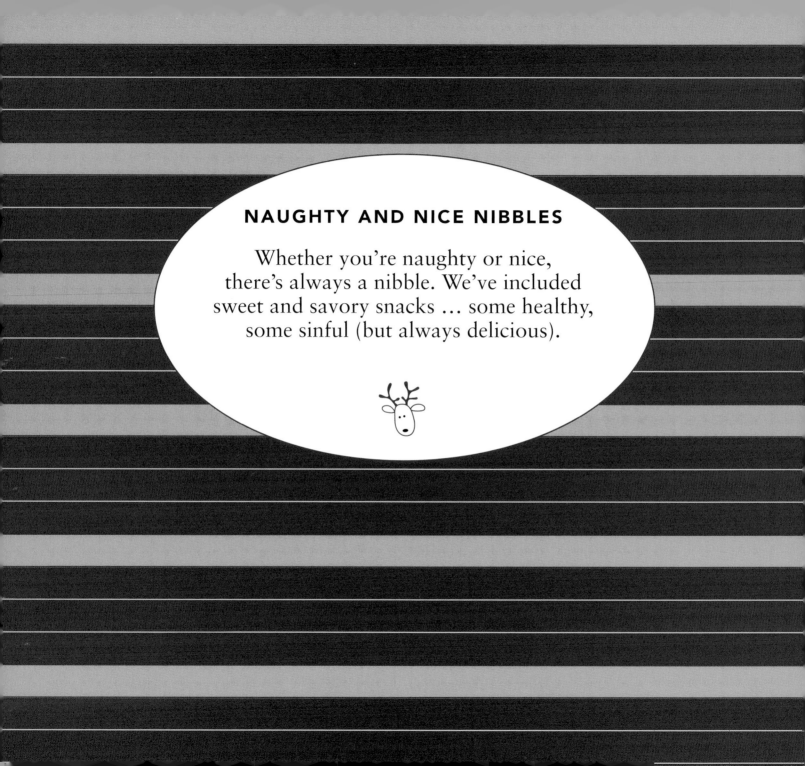

BAGEL RINGS
Bagels with Assorted Toppings

Although these speedy snacks are as simple as can be, remember that simplicity doesn't make them any less fun or delicious. You can be as creative as you want with the extras. We've tried chocolate chips; red, yellow, and green bell peppers; apricots and blueberries; the list goes on and on…. This version is a berry, pinecone, and mint bow version.

½ cup chopped walnuts

6 plain bagels, halved

8 ounces whipped cream cheese

½ cup chopped dried cranberries

½ cup pitted and chopped dates

12 fresh mint sprigs

❋ **Preheat the oven** to 375 degrees F.

❋ **Place the walnuts** in a pie tin. Put the tin in the oven, and toast the nuts until toasted and fragrant, about 5 minutes. Cool.

❋ **Lightly toast the bagel halves.** Spread the bagels with the cream cheese.

❋ **In 3 small bowls,** place the cranberries, walnuts, and dates.

❋ **Take your bagel** and dress it up with the various toppings. Add the mint sprig for your final "bow" garnish.

SERVES 6

BLIXEN'S MIX
Personalized Gorp

Bowls of healthy, crunchy munchies are great to have around for the holidays. Fill your gorp with your family's favorite fruits and nuts … and if you're in a sinful mood (well, it is the holidays) add any kind of chocolate chips you desire.

1 cup salted banana chips

1 cup coarsely chopped walnuts

½ cup mini chocolate chips

½ cup sweetened dried cranberries

½ cup dried blueberries

½ cup coarsely chopped dried apricots

½ teaspoon sea salt

In a large bowl, combine all the ingredients and toss several times. Store in a tightly sealed container for up to 1 week.

MAKES 4 CUPS

SKATER'S DIP
Buttermilk Ranch Dipping Sauce with Cauliflower, Snap Peas, Carrots, and Cucumber

The dip is creamy and smooth, and boy do those veggies taste divine! Dunk your choice of vegetables into this rich, flavorful sauce. We like to dip snap peas, Persian cucumbers, baby carrots, and cauliflower, but all crunchy vegetables work.

DIPPING SAUCE

½ cup buttermilk

½ cup sour cream

1 medium clove garlic

1½ tablespoons fresh lemon juice

Pinch sugar

Dash Worcestershire sauce

Salt and freshly ground black pepper

1 teaspoon lemon zest

8 ounces snap peas

4 Persian cucumbers

1 pound baby carrots

1 head cauliflower

To make the dipping sauce: Combine the buttermilk, sour cream, garlic, lemon juice, sugar, and Worcestershire in a blender or food processor fitted with a steel blade. Blend until smooth. Transfer into a bowl, and add salt and pepper to taste. Sprinkle with the lemon zest.

Clean all the vegetables. Pull the ends off the peas, halve and cut the cucumbers into thirds lengthwise, cut the ends off the carrots, and cut the cauliflower into florets.

Arrange the vegetables on a large plate or platter. Place the dip in the center, and serve.

MAKES 1 CUP; SERVES 6

REINDEER BARK
Chocolate-Almond Bark

Oh, what a treat this makes! You and your family won't believe that making such a coveted gift item (or sweet treat) could take such little time. Feel free to change the type of chocolate and nuts to customize your bark.

1¼ cups whole raw almonds

1 tablespoon olive oil

¼ teaspoon fine sea salt

6 ounces bittersweet chocolate, finely chopped

6 ounces milk chocolate, finely chopped

Preheat the oven to 375 degrees F.

In a medium bowl, combine the almonds, olive oil, and sea salt. Spread them on a rimmed baking sheet. Bake until toasted and fragrant, 8 to 10 minutes. Set aside.

Turn the oven down to 250 degrees F.

Line a 17 x 11-inch rimmed baking sheet with parchment paper. Spread both kinds of chopped chocolate all over the sheet. Place in the oven until soft, about 5 minutes. Remove from the oven and spread the chocolate with a spatula or dull knife evenly to the edges. Immediately sprinkle with the toasted and salted almonds. Bury the nuts in the chocolate. Refrigerate the bark for 2 to 3 hours, and then cut it into bite-sized pieces. Wrap in parchment and store in a plastic container in the refrigerator 2 to 3 weeks.

MAKES 1 POUND

SNOW ANGEL
Toast Cutout with Egg and Freshly Grated Parmesan

There's the classic "egg in a hole," but how about an egg in an angel or a snowman or a reindeer or a star? Now you can create any one your child desires. In fact, let the kids choose the cookie cutter and do the cutting of the buttered toast.

1 tablespoon plus
½ teaspoon butter

1 large egg

Salt and freshly ground
black pepper

1 slice bread

In a small saucepan over medium heat, melt 1 tablespoon of the butter. When the butter begins to bubble, gently crack the egg right into the middle of the pan. Add salt and pepper to taste to the egg. While the egg is cooking, place your bread in the toaster. Let the egg cook for 2 minutes, then cover for another 1 to 1½ minutes. Check to see that the edges of the white are crispy, and that the rest of the white looks fully cooked. Place the cooked egg on a plate.

Use the remaining ½ teaspoon butter on the toast. Place it on a cutting board. Press an angel or other cookie cutter into the center of the buttered toast. Pull the shape out. Place the toast with the angel-shaped hole over the fried egg. Place the angel to the side.

SERVES 1

SUGARPLUM LOLLIES
Chocolate-Dipped Marshmallows with Assorted Toppings

Sugarplum fairies, sugarplum treats, and now, yes it's true … sugarplum pops! These bright, sweet treats are a great gift wrapped in cellophane with a bow, or clustered into a little sugarplum bouquet—perfect for Grandma.

Nonstick vegetable or canola oil spray

12 ounces bittersweet chocolate chips

Toppings: assorted sprinkles, colored sugars, nuts, flaked coconut, chips (white, peanut butter, or milk chocolate mini), coarsely chopped candy canes

1 (10-ounce) bag large marshmallows

20 wooden craft/Popsicle sticks

Line a cookie sheet with parchment paper. Lightly spray it with oil, then wipe the oil evenly across the parchment.

Place the chocolate in the top of a double boiler or in a metal bowl over a saucepan filled with 1 inch of hot water (creating your own double boiler). Melt the chocolate chips over medium-low heat until smooth, about 8 minutes. Transfer the melted chocolate to a room temperature bowl.

Put each topping ingredient in a separate, shallow bowl.

Stab each marshmallow with a craft stick, securing the marshmallow on the top (pushing the stick in about 1 inch), creating a lollipop. Dip the marshmallow pop into the chocolate and cover it evenly. Dip it into the various toppings. Put the marshmallow pop on the parchment to set. Repeat.

Refrigerate the marshmallow pops until the chocolate has completely hardened, at least 45 minutes.

MAKES 20 POPS

SLEIGH RIDER CIDER
Apple-Raspberry Spiced Cider

Here's a healthy alternative to all the sugary holiday punches. The frozen raspberries and blackberries give a nice surprising tart burst of flavor.

2 quarts apple cider

1 (16-ounce) can frozen raspberry cocktail concentrate, thawed

2 cinnamon sticks

1 cup frozen blackberries, thawed

1 cup frozen raspberries, thawed

In a stockpot over medium-high heat, combine the cider, raspberry concentrate, and cinnamon sticks. Bring the mixture to a simmer and heat for 8 to 10 minutes, so that it's warm through. Add the berries.

Let the berries cook for 2 minutes. Stir. Pour into festive heat-resistant glasses or mugs.

SERVES 8 TO 10

CHIMNEY CAKES
Assorted Mini Loaves

These make delightful presents for friends and family! Just wrap them in bright cellophane, secure with a bow, and your gift is complete. You can use this basic recipe for a multitude of variations. Here we made two plain, two cinnamon, and two lemon–chocolate chip.

12 ounces (3 sticks) unsalted butter, at room temperature

1½ cups sugar

6 large eggs

1½ teaspoons vanilla extract

2 cups sifted all-purpose flour

¼ cup sour cream

CINNAMON NUT (PER 2 CAKES)

½ cup chopped pecans

2 teaspoons ground cinnamon

LEMON–CHOCOLATE CHIP (PER 2 CAKES)

1 teaspoon lemon zest

2 teaspoons lemon juice

½ cup chocolate chips

6 tablespoons powdered sugar

Preheat the oven to 325 degrees F. Line six 6 x 3-inch loaf pans with waxed paper.

In a medium bowl, beat the butter until fluffy. Gradually add the sugar, keeping the mixture fluffy.

In a large bowl, beat the eggs. Add the butter mixture, beating until light and fluffy. Stir in the vanilla. Stir in the flour and sour cream; continue to beat until smooth.

Fill 2 pans ¾ full with the basic recipe, then divide the remaining batter in half and use your choice of mix-ins.

Place the pans in the oven and bake until the edges separate from the pan, about 55 minutes. The mini loaves should be golden on top. Cool on a rack for 15 to 20 minutes. Remove from the baking pans and sprinkle with powdered sugar.

MAKES 6 MINI LOAVES

CELEBRATION STICKS
Colored Chocolate-Dipped Pretzels

Tailor these festive sticks to your family's special celebration. You can use semisweet chocolate or white chocolate as the base for the colored sprinkles.

Sprinkles (colors depending on the holiday)

1 cup white chocolate chips or semisweet chocolate chips

15 (8-inch) pretzel rods

Raffia or ribbon

Arrange 1¼-inch waxed paper strips of whichever colors of sprinkles you intend to use (red/green/white or blue/white/blue or red/green/black, etc.).

Place the chocolate chips in the top of a double boiler or a metal bowl over a saucepan filled with 1 inch of hot water (creating your own double boiler). Melt the chocolate chips over medium-low heat until smooth, about 8 minutes.

Use a butter knife to spread the chocolate over half of a pretzel.

Roll the pretzel over the sprinkle strips until coated. Repeat with the remaining pretzels. Place them on a baking sheet covered in waxed paper. Refrigerate for 30 minutes. Tie the pretzels into little bunches with colorful raffia or ribbon.

MAKES 15 STICKS

NEW YEAR'S NUGGETS
Chocolate-Caramel Popcorn

You thought caramel corn was just right the way it was … well, maybe this drizzled chocolate variety will quickly change your mind. It makes a wonderful gift, wrapped in a festive bag or placed in a colorful tin. In our families we refer to this yummy treat as Grandpa's Delight.

½ cup dried yellow popcorn
3 tablespoons canola oil (optional)
1 cup sugar
½ cup light corn syrup

Scant ¼ cup water
¼ teaspoon orange extract (optional)
8 ounces milk chocolate

❋ **Pop the popcorn** in an air popper or in a large stockpot. If you use a stockpot, place the canola oil in the pot and heat over medium heat for about 1 minute. Add the popcorn, covering the bottom of the pan with an even layer of kernels. Cover the pan and let the kernels heat until they begin to pop vigorously, 1 to 2 minutes. Shake the pan every 15 seconds so that kernels will not burn. The corn should finish popping in 3 to 4 minutes.

❋ **Line several cookie sheets** with parchment paper.

❋ **In a heavy-bottomed saucepan,** combine the sugar, corn syrup, and water. Heat over medium-high heat until golden brown, about 5 minutes. Stir gently, add the orange extract, if using, stir again. Add some of the popcorn and coat it with the caramel. Use a wooden utensil to help coat the corn. Place the coated kernels on the parchment paper to cool. Repeat.

❋ **When cool,** break up the clumps of caramel corn, keeping the corn clumps on the parchment.

❋ **Heat the chocolate** over low heat in the top of a double boiler, or in a metal bowl over a saucepan filled with 1 inch of hot water (creating your own double boiler). Heat the chocolate until it's smooth, 3 to 4 minutes. Make sure the chocolate doesn't burn.

❋ **Fill a ladle** with the melted chocolate and lightly drizzle over the caramel corn. Let the chocolate caramel corn cool for 30 to 45 minutes. To make gifts, put small batches in cellophane bags; otherwise, wrap in parchment paper and keep in a Tupperware container in the refrigerator for 3 to 5 days.

MAKES 4 CUPS

HEAVENLY COOKIES
Holiday Shortbread

These cookies are nothing "short" of heavenly! Dried apricots, toasted pecans, chocolate chunks, and the like can be chopped into small pieces and placed in the mixer along with the rest of the ingredients. A teaspoon of ground ginger or cinnamon will also pack a subtle punch!

2½ cups all-purpose flour

10 ounces (2½ sticks) cold unsalted butter, cut into small pieces

½ cup powdered sugar

Pinch salt

¼ teaspoon vanilla extract

In a stand mixer, combine the flour, butter, sugar, and salt. Using the paddle attachment, mix the ingredients on low speed until combined. Add the vanilla. Mix until the dough is smooth and comes together.

Turn the dough out onto a floured work surface. Divide into 2 pieces. On the edge of a piece of parchment or waxed paper, shape the dough into a log, and carefully roll up until the paper ends, folding the outside corners into the log. Repeat with the second piece of dough. Refrigerate for at least 30 minutes.

Preheat the oven to 275 degrees F.

Remove the rolled logs, unwrap, and cut into ¼-inch slices. Transfer to ungreased cookie sheets and bake until golden on the edges, about 25 minutes. Transfer the cookies to wire racks to cool for 15 to 20 minutes before handling.

MAKES 50 COOKIES

SWEET SOMETHINGS

It's crunchy, it's chewy, it's buttery,
and it's yummy! Whether you're in the
mood for fancy, decorated cupcakes, or
good old-fashioned buttery cookies,
we've got you covered.

SWEET SNOW
Vanilla Ice Cream with Tasty Add-Ins

We don't think there's a soul who doesn't love the taste of pure, clean vanilla ice cream. So here's a simple recipe to make with family and friends. Of course, if plain vanilla seems a little too conventional, we've got a handful of decadent add-ins that will transform your classic flavor into your very own customized creamy mix.

ICE CREAM

1½ cups whole milk

1 vanilla bean, split lengthwise

¾ cup sugar

⅛ teaspoon salt

2 large egg yolks

2 cups heavy cream

ADD-INS

1 cup coarsely chopped chocolate peppermints

1½ cups dried tart cherries plus ½ cup bittersweet chocolate chips

1 cup coarsely chopped Heath bars

¾ cup coarsely chopped candy canes

1 cup coarsely chopped Reese's peanut butter cups

In a medium saucepan, heat the milk over low heat until bubbles form around the edges of the pan. Scrape the seeds from the vanilla bean into the milk. Add the bean to the pan. Stir the milk for 1 to 2 minutes. Stir in the sugar and salt until dissolved. Remove from the heat and let cool for 10 minutes.

In a small stainless-steel bowl, beat the egg yolks until blended. Gradually whisk in the milk mixture until combined. Remove the vanilla bean. Set the bowl over a saucepan of barely simmering water. Cook, stirring constantly, until the mixture is thick enough to coat the back of a spoon, 10 to 12 minutes. Remove from the heat, stir in the cream, then cover and refrigerate until completely cool. Freeze in an ice cream maker according to the manufacturer's instructions. When the ice cream base is nearly frozen, add the add-ins and continue freezing.

Store frozen for up to 1 week.

MAKES 1 QUART

FROSTY AND FRIENDS
Marshmallow Snowman

Marshmallow snowmen are perfect treats for little hands to make. Young kids might love making Frosty come to life so much that they may choose not to devour him (but we doubt it)! Make just one or make half a dozen—the only place they'll melt is in a smiling mouth!

3 large marshmallows
3 toothpicks
Royal Icing (page 59)
Miniature chocolate chips

1 pretzel stick (small and thin)
8 inches skinny red licorice (or fruit leather cut into a thin strip)
1 Hershey's Kiss or Rollo candy

Connect 2 marshmallows on the first toothpick. Push the second toothpick halfway into the top of the second marshmallow and spike your third marshmallow onto the top half of the toothpick. The toothpicks should be completely hidden in the marshmallows.

Using your third toothpick as a glue stick, add dots of icing to stick on chocolate chips to form "eyes" and "buttons." Break the pretzel stick in half for arms, and carefully push them into the sides of the middle marshmallow. Wrap the licorice (or fruit leather) around the "neck" for a scarf, and use icing to glue the Kiss or Rollo onto Frosty's head as a hat.

MAKES 1 SNOWMAN

TIP For a small table centerpiece, scoop a few mounds of Royal Icing onto a cake platter. Before the icing dries, cut a few red braided licorice sticks into thirds to make skis for Frosty and his friends. Place the skis on the icing mounds, under 3 or 4 marshmallow snowmen. Anchor the snowmen onto the skis using half a pretzel stick.

REINDEER PRINTS
Butter Cookies with Colored Sugar

We decided to give you a larger recipe for these lovely, flavorful butter cookies since they are the perfect cookies to decorate for any holiday. Kids will have fun designing chocolate chip "paw prints" into the cookies. And by the way, they are delicious without any trimmings, so feel free to bake them plain if you're looking for a delicious, buttery morsel to have with a cup of tea or hot cocoa.

8 ounces (2 sticks) unsalted butter, at room temperature

1 cup sugar

1½ tablespoons heavy cream

2 large egg yolks

1½ teaspoons vanilla extract

¼ teaspoon almond extract

2¼ cups flour

⅛ teaspoon baking powder

¼ teaspoon salt

Chocolate chips, dried fruit, chocolate candies, or colored sugar for decorating

Royal Icing (page 59), for decorating (optional)

Preheat the oven to 350 degrees F.

In a large bowl, beat together the butter and sugar until fluffy. Add the cream, egg yolks, vanilla, and almond extract and mix thoroughly. Add the flour, baking powder, and salt and combine. Shape the dough into a disk, wrap in plastic, and place in the refrigerator for ½ hour. Lightly flour a flat surface, dust a rolling pin, and roll out the dough to ⅛ inch thick.

Begin cutting the dough into shapes and decorate with chocolate chips, dried fruit, or candies, or sprinkle with colored sugar.

Place onto ungreased cookie sheets 1 inch apart and bake until the edges are golden, 8 to 11 minutes. Transfer to cooling racks and let cool completely before adding the icing, if using.

MAKES 60 COOKIES

CONVERSION TA'
1 inch = 2.54 cm
2 inches = 5.08 cm
ches = 7.62 cm
= 10 16 cm
.70 cm
cm

SANTA'S TREATS
Chocolate, Cherry, and Coconut Oatmeal Cookies

We threw a few of our favorite tastes together—chocolate, cherries, and coconut—to create this sensational oatmeal cookie. We suggest rationing these one plate at a time; otherwise, they'll be gone as soon as you take them out of the oven!

1 cup all-purpose flour

½ cup old-fashioned rolled oats

½ teaspoon baking soda

¼ teaspoon baking powder

½ teaspoon salt

4½ ounces (1 stick plus 1 tablespoon) unsalted butter, at room temperature

¾ cup packed light brown sugar

1 large egg

½ teaspoon vanilla extract

½ cup chocolate chips

½ cup unsweetened shredded coconut

¼ cup dried tart cherries

Ice cream, for serving (optional)

☃ **Preheat the oven** to 350 degrees F.

☃ **In a large bowl,** blend together the flour, oats, baking soda, baking powder, and salt. In another large bowl, beat together 4 ounces of the butter and the sugar until fluffy. Beat in the egg, then add the vanilla. Add the flour mixture, incorporating it completely. Stir in the chocolate chips, coconut, and cherries.

☃ **Grease 2 baking sheets lightly** with the remaining 1 tablespoon butter. Take 1-tablespoon portions of batter and drop them onto the cookie sheets 2 to 2½ inches apart. Bake the cookies until perfectly golden brown, 12 to 15 minutes. Cool the cookies on racks, or serve warm with ice cream.

MAKES 3 DOZEN COOKIES

SANTA'S STEAMER
Minty Hot Chocolate

Ho, Ho, Ho!!! Here's a tantalizing spin on a classic. Add a little holiday touch by hanging mini candy canes on the sides of the mugs.

5 cups whole milk

1 cup heavy cream

4½ tablespoons sugar

3 tablespoons unsweetened cocoa powder

½ teaspoon peppermint extract

In a medium saucepan, whisk together the milk, cream, sugar, and cocoa. Heat over medium-low heat until simmering, 2 to 3 minutes. Add the peppermint extract and whisk continuously for 1 minute, frothing the liquid. When the mint chocolate is nice and frothy, pour evenly into 6 mugs, and serve.

SERVES 6

ICE CREAM TREEWITCHES
Ice Cream Sandwiches

These Christmas tree–shaped ice cream sandwiches are spiked with a little touch of cinnamon, which gives them a special festive flavor. These are great, tasty creations for the whole family, so grab your mother, father, aunt, or uncle and start baking! Feel free to use other large ornamental cookie cutters if you'd like to make a variety of ice cream sandwiches.

3 cups all-purpose flour, plus more as needed

2 tablespoons unsweetened cocoa powder

1 teaspoon baking powder

1 teaspoon ground cinnamon (optional)

Pinch salt

1 cup sugar

8 ounces (2 sticks) unsalted butter, at room temperature, plus enough to grease baking sheets

1 large egg, lightly beaten

1 tablespoon milk

1 teaspoon vanilla extract

2½ cups Vanilla Ice Cream (page 49)

❄ **In a small bowl,** combine the flour, cocoa, baking powder, cinnamon, if desired, and salt; set aside. In a large bowl, beat the sugar and butter together until creamy. Add the egg, milk, and vanilla. Gradually beat in the flour mixture just until combined. Shape the dough into 2 disks and wrap in plastic. Refrigerate for 2 to 3 hours, or overnight.

❄ **Preheat the oven** to 375 degrees F. Lightly grease 2 baking sheets.

❄ **Lightly flour a work surface** and roll out 1 disk of dough to ⅛ inch thick, adding flour as necessary and turning the dough to prevent sticking. Cut with a 4 x 4-inch cookie cutter (such as a Christmas tree).

Bake until the centers are set, 8 to 10 minutes. Repeat to make the second batch.

❄ **Let the cookies stand** on the baking sheets for 1 to 2 minutes. Remove from baking sheets to a wire rack; cool.

❄ **Soften the ice cream** for a few minutes in the refrigerator. Spread a thick layer of ice cream (about 4 tablespoons) on half of the cookies. Make sure the layer is smooth. Top with the other cookies and press together lightly. Gobble immediately, or wrap in foil and freeze for up to 3 months.

SERVES 10

What would the holidays be without gingerbread girls and boys? These yummy cookies are fun to make, eat, and give away. Invite a group of friends over and have a Gingerbread People party! The Royal Icing used in this recipe dries very hard, making these cookies suitable for packaging or wrapping to freeze. Colored sugars, mini chocolate chips, Red Hots, and sprinkles bring these characters to life! We've created a recipe using meringue powder, rather than egg whites, as it is more suitable for small children (for food safety). Meringue powder can be purchased in the baking supply section of many craft stores or at www.wilton.com.

GINGERBREAD PEOPLE

6 cups sifted all-purpose flour

1 teaspoon baking soda

½ teaspoon baking powder

8 ounces (2 sticks) unsalted butter, at room temperature

1 cup packed dark brown sugar

4 teaspoons ground ginger

1¼ teaspoons ground cloves

1 teaspoon salt

¼ teaspoon finely ground black pepper

1 cup unsulfered molasses

2 large eggs

ROYAL ICING

1 pound (about 4 cups) powdered sugar

6 tablespoons warm water

3 tablespoons meringue powder

Piping bag with small round tip

Decorations, such as Red Hots, mini chocolate chips, colored sugar, or chocolate sprinkles

☃ **To make the Gingerbread People:** In a large bowl, sift together the flour, baking soda, and baking powder. Set aside.

☃ **In a mixer on medium-high speed,** beat the butter and brown sugar until fluffy. Mix in the ginger, cloves, salt, and pepper, then the molasses and eggs. Add the flour mixture; combine on low speed just until the flour is incorporated. Divide the dough into thirds, and wrap each piece in plastic. Chill for at least 1 hour.

☃ **Preheat the oven** to 350 degrees F.

☃ **On a floured work surface,** roll the dough ⅛ inch thick. Using cookie cutters of various sizes, cut out

continued ⋯>

your gingerbread people! Transfer to ungreased baking sheets, and bake until crisp, 8 to 10 minutes. Let the cookies cool on wire racks for 20 minutes before decorating.

☃ **To make the Royal Icing:** In a mixer, beat the powdered sugar, water, and meringue powder on low speed for 1 minute. Increase the speed to medium, and continue beating until the icing forms soft peaks, 6 to 8 minutes. For a thinner icing, add ½ teaspoon additional water at a time until you reach your desired consistency.

☃ **Working quickly,** transfer enough icing to fill half a piping bag. Twist the bag to close and secure with a kitchen tie. Cover the surface of the rest of the icing with a slightly damp kitchen towel until refilling the bag, or cover and refrigerate for later use. (Makes 3 cups.)

☃ **Decorating your Christmas buddy** can be as simple as a few dots of Royal Icing, or as fancy as you like. Red Hots and mini chocolate chips are old favorites, while colored sugar sprinkled on top of freshly piped icing can be used to add wonderful color and texture. Cookies will take approximately 30 minutes to set. Store cookies in a large Tupperware container by laying them flat between sheets of parchment or waxed paper. At room temperature, they will last up to 1 week; refrigerated, 2 weeks; and frozen, 3 months.

MAKES ABOUT 2 DOZEN COOKIES

NORTH POLE DELIGHTS
Six-Layer Bars

This may be an old favorite, but it's a goody. This simple, scrumptious dessert is a perfect holiday treat for every member of the family. Our "big kid" husbands can't keep their hands off them.

4 ounces (1 stick) unsalted butter

3½ cups graham cracker crumbs

1 cup semisweet chocolate chips

1 cup dried tart cherries

1 cup chopped pecans

1 (14-ounce) can sweetened condensed milk

1 cup shredded sweetened coconut

Preheat the oven to 375 degrees F.

Melt the butter in a small saucepan over medium heat.

Grease a 13 x 9-inch baking pan with a little of the butter, making sure to get all the corners and sides.

Stir the graham cracker crumbs and remaining butter together in the baking pan. Spread the crumb mixture and pat it down, creating an even crust. Layer the chocolate chips, cherries, and pecans evenly over the graham crust. Pour the sweetened condensed milk over the top. Finish with an even sprinkle of coconut.

Bake until the bars are lightly golden on top, 25 to 30 minutes. Remove the pan to a wire rack to cool completely before cutting into 2 x 2-inch squares. Store in an airtight container for 3 to 5 days.

MAKES 36 BARS

SANTA'S SECRET STASH
Buttery Ball Cookies

These are Jessica's son Lucian's favorite holiday cookie. In fact, he makes a special stash for himself so that the rest of the family doesn't eat them all before he's gotten his fill.

4 ounces (1 stick) unsalted butter, at room temperature, plus extra for greasing cookie sheet

4 tablespoons honey

1 cup unbleached all-purpose flour

1 tablespoon vanilla extract

½ teaspoon salt

1¼ cups finely chopped pecans

1 cup powdered sugar

Preheat the oven to 300 degrees F. Grease a cookie sheet.

Using a mixer, beat the butter until soft. Beat in the honey, then slowly add the flour, vanilla, and salt. Add the pecans and mix until incorporated. Form the dough into a ball and cover it in plastic wrap. Place in the refrigerator and chill for 1 to 2 hours.

Transfer the chilled dough to a clean work surface and, using your hands, form quarter-sized balls and place them one inch apart on the prepared cookie sheet. Bake until golden, about 40 minutes. Remove from the oven and let cool slightly, 5 to 10 minutes. Dust and roll the warm balls in the powdered sugar, let stand for 10 minutes, and roll again.

Store in an airtight container for up to 1 week.

MAKES ABOUT 3 DOZEN COOKIES

INCREDIBLE EDIBLE ORNAMENTS
Decorative Cupcakes

These Christmas ornaments look good enough to eat and, lucky for you, they are! Let your imagination run wild with these cupcakes and decorate them any way that feels festive to you. We have chosen a nontraditional, but nonetheless delicious Peanut Butter–Chocolate Chip Cupcake recipe with Cream Cheese Icing, but you can use any favorite cupcake or frosting recipe. As beautiful as these look, they're not really meant to hang on a tree.

Cupcake or muffin pan

Paper cupcake liners

Piping bag with small round tip or plastic Ziploc bag

PEANUT BUTTER–CHOCOLATE CHIP CUPCAKES

1 cup all-purpose flour

1 teaspoon baking powder

½ teaspoon salt

⅔ cup smooth peanut butter

½ cup packed light brown sugar

2⅓ ounces (½ stick plus ½ tablespoon) unsalted butter, at room temperature

2 large eggs

1 teaspoon vanilla extract

⅓ cup milk

1¼ cups semisweet chocolate chips

CREAM CHEESE ICING

8 ounces cream cheese, at room temperature

4 ounces (1 stick) unsalted butter, at room temperature

3½ cups powdered sugar, sifted

1 teaspoon vanilla extract

Food coloring (pick 2 fun colors)

Colorful chocolate-coated candies

12 thin twisted pretzels

12 mini peanut butter cups

❋ **Preheat the oven** to 350 degrees F. Line the muffin pan with paper liners.

❋ **To make the cupcakes:** In a large bowl, sift together the flour, baking powder, and salt and set aside. With a mixer, beat together the peanut butter, brown sugar, and butter until smooth and well blended. Add the eggs, 1 at a time, beating well after each addition, until the mixture is thick and glossy. Stir in the vanilla. Alternate folding in the flour and milk, a little at a time, until well blended. Fold in the chocolate chips.

continued ···>

✳ **Fill the prepared muffin cups** ¾ full and bake until a knife or toothpick inserted in the center comes out clean, 20 to 30 minutes.

✳ **Cool the cupcakes** in the pan for 10 minutes before removing. Cool on a wire rack for 20 more minutes before beginning to frost.

✳ **To make the icing:** With a mixer, beat the cream cheese and butter on low speed until combined, about 30 seconds. Slowly add the powdered sugar, a little at a time, until the sugar is well incorporated, about 1 minute. Add the vanilla. Increase the mixer to medium speed, and mix the icing until fluffy, about 1 more minute.

✳ **To assemble:** Color your frosting: Separate the frosting into 2 batches: ⅔ of your batch for frosting the cupcakes and ⅓ of your batch for piping decorations. Mix food coloring 1 drop at a time into the first batch, mixing well after each addition, until you reach your desired color. Using a second color, do the same for the second batch.

✳ **Using a knife or small plastic spatula,** frost the cupcakes.

✳ **Using the second batch of frosting,** fill a prepared piping bag or Ziploc bag halfway full. If using a Ziploc bag, cut the very tip of one of the corners of the bag, and it will serve as a piping bag.

✳ **With your piping bag** and colorful candies, decorate your cupcakes.

✳ **Break the pretzels** to resemble small hooks. Insert a broken-off pretzel piece into the bottom of a mini peanut butter cup. Repeat with the 11 remaining pretzels and peanut butter cups.

✳ **Top each cupcake** with your "hooks" and voilà! Your edible ornament is complete. These are meant to be eaten right away. If you're having a party, they can be given as treats, but should also be eaten within a day or two.

MAKES 12 CUPCAKES

MRS. CLAUS'S PEPPERMINT WONDERS
Chocolate-Mint Brownies

Mint, chocolate, chewy, decadent, and simply delightful … those are just a few words to describe these sumptuous treats. If only we could bottle the smell of them baking!

BROWNIES

¾ cup chopped walnuts

8 ounces (2 sticks) unsalted butter

5 ounces semisweet chocolate, chopped

2 ounces unsweetened chocolate, chopped

1 cup granulated sugar

1½ teaspoons vanilla extract

½ teaspoon salt

2 large eggs

7 tablespoons all-purpose flour

FROSTING

2 cups powdered sugar, sifted

4 ounces (1 stick) unsalted butter, at room temperature

2 tablespoons whole milk

6 large candy canes, crushed into pieces

8 ounces semisweet chocolate chips

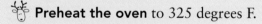 **Preheat the oven** to 325 degrees F.

To make the brownies: Grease an 8- or 9-inch square baking pan. Line the bottom of the pan with aluminum foil, allowing extra to hang over the sides.

Spread the walnuts on a baking sheet and bake until toasted and fragrant, 10 to 12 minutes. Remove from the oven and let cool.

In a double boiler over barely simmering water or in a metal bowl over a saucepan filled with 1 inch of hot water (creating your own double boiler), melt the butter and chocolates together, stirring often. Remove from the heat and allow to cool for about 10 minutes.

Stir in the granulated sugar, vanilla, and salt until well blended. Whisk in the eggs one at a time. Stir in the flour until well blended. Stir in the walnuts.

Spread in the prepared pan and bake until a toothpick inserted in the center comes out clean, about 35 minutes. The top should be puffy and shiny and cracked. Remove from the oven and let cool in the pan for 1 hour.

Lift the contents from the pan using the foil and invert onto a plate. Carefully remove the foil and turn the cake rightside up. Cool.

To make the frosting: In a medium bowl, mix the powdered sugar, butter, and milk until creamy.

Spread the brownies with the frosting, then sprinkle with candy cane pieces and chocolate chips. Chill for 45 minutes to 1 hour. Cut into 20 small squares.

MAKES 20 SMALL BROWNIES

CHUNKS O' CHOCOLATE
Chocolate Truffles

These black and white truffles are rich, dense, and superchocolaty. Pop them in your mouth after you dip them into their cocoa or powdered-sugar coating, or decorate boxes (see page 72) with your friends and your brothers and sisters and tuck these sweet little morsels inside for a lovely holiday gift.

8 ounces semisweet chocolate, coarsely chopped

½ cup heavy cream

2 tablespoons vanilla extract

¼ cup unsweetened cocoa powder, sifted

¼ cup powdered sugar, sifted

✳ **Place the chocolate** in a medium, heat-resistant bowl. In a small saucepan, heat the cream, bringing it to a boil. Pour the cream over the chocolate and let sit for 5 minutes. Stir the mixture until smooth. Add the vanilla and blend completely.

✳ **Cover the bowl** with plastic wrap and refrigerate until firm, 3 to 4 hours.

✳ **Cover a cookie sheet** with parchment paper. Place the cocoa and powdered sugar in separate, shallow bowls.

✳ **Take a teaspoon** of the hardened truffle dough in your hand. Roll it quickly between your palms, making it into a completely round ball. Drop it in either the cocoa or the powdered sugar, and roll until fully coated. Repeat with the remaining truffle dough.

✳ **Place the truffles** on the parchment paper and chill until hard, 1 to 2 hours.

✳ **Store in an airtight container** for up to 2 weeks.

MAKES 30 TRUFFLES

TIP To make with nuts, use ¼ cup chopped walnuts or pecans and add the nuts to the cookie sheet before rolling the truffles.

HAPPY HOLIDAY WORKSHOP

Grab a group of friends and make like
Santa's elves. With all these fabulous and
easy-to-make crafts, you'll have your home
decorated and plenty of beautiful
handmade gifts to give.

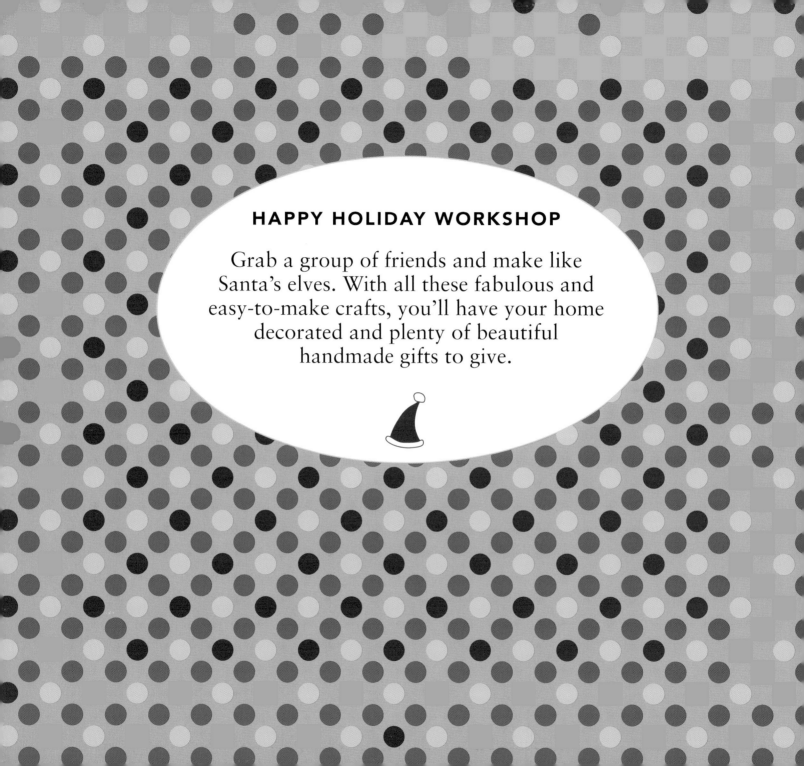

PICTURE PAL
Twig Photo Frame

Holiday photos deserve a frame as special as the moment they've captured. This beautiful frame made from found twigs is truly unique and looks wonderful with any decor. Make a few and hang as a triptych, with the center frame larger than the two on either side.

Hot-glue gun

1 photo for framing

Ruler

Scissors

Colored construction paper

12 to 16 twigs, 8 to 15 inches long (depending on the size of your photo)

Garden shears

Twine or string

Twisty ties (optional)

Glue your photo onto the center of a piece of construction paper that complements your photo. Draw a line on the paper 1 inch around the photo and cut around it. This will create a 1-inch border.

Divide your twigs into 2 groups. Half of them should be 3 inches taller than your photo; the other half should be 3 inches wider than your photo. Use garden shears to trim them to the correct lengths.

Using 3 or 4 twigs per side, arrange them so that they surround the bordered photo and extend outward about an inch in each direction. Bind the twigs at each corner using twine or string, making an X pattern. (Using a twisty tie can really help hold the corners in place while you are tying the twigs.)

On to the back of your twig frame, dot glue on each of the corners, and attach your photo, faceside down, so that when you turn the frame around, it is centered.

Glue a small loop of string to the center back of the twig frame for hanging the photo.

MAKES 1 FRAMED PHOTO

TASTY TREASURES
Beaded Box of Holiday Shortbread

Sparkling beads make a beautiful presentation for this holiday box that you can fill with cookies like scrumptious shortbreads (page 46). The jeweled box is a fun-to-make keepsake for a special friend, teacher, or family member.

Newspaper

6 x 6 x 4-inch craft box (natural color or white)

Assorted beads, such as rhinestones (any bead with a flat bottom is fine)

Good-quality craft glue

Parchment or waxed paper

☃ **On a work surface** spread with newspaper, take the top off of the craft box, and set the bottom of the box aside. On the top of the box, you can either draw a design in pencil to which the beads can then be glued, you can glue a pattern of colored beads in straight rows, or you can randomly cover the box top with your jewels! Really, anything goes!

☃ **When you have finished,** let the glue set for about 2 hours so that the jewels are firmly set. Now you can line the bottom and sides of the box with a large piece of parchment or waxed paper. The paper should be long enough to hang over the sides of the box.

☃ **Fill the box with cookies,** folding the overhanging paper over the top. Place the box top on, and your gift is complete!

MAKES 1 BOX

TIP These boxes are a very versatile craft. Buttons, beads, pieces of ribbon (you name it!) will all work beautifully. Pom-poms add a fun dimension and contrast nicely with rhinestones.

SANTA'S SUDS
Decorated Soap

These customized bars of soap are a perfect project for kids of all ages. Beware: grown-ups may not be able to keep their hands off this one, either! Wrap three bars together in clear cellophane, tie with ribbon, and you've got a wonderful gift to give, not to mention clean hands all around!

Acrylic paints
Paper cups
Paintbrushes

New bars of white or glycerine soap
Coffee can or disposable mini loaf pan

Large pot
Canning wax or a white candle

🎅 **Squeeze a different color of paint** into each paper cup. You can use as many colors or as few as you like.

🎅 **Using a different paintbrush for each color,** paint designs on the "face" of the soap with the acrylics. You can make a background by painting a solid color over the whole face, letting it dry for about 10 minutes, and then painting your design (Christmas tree, dreidel, heart, monogram, etc.) right on top.

🎅 **While the design dries,** put the coffee can or loaf pan in a large pot half-filled with hot water. Drop the wax into the can (or loaf pan), and melt it over medium-low heat.

🎅 **Seal it!** When the wax has melted, use a disposable paintbrush to lightly cover your dried design with wax. One or two even layers is sufficient; more will cloud the painting. The wax coating allows the soap to be used again and again without washing your design away!

MAKES MULTIPLE SOAPS

TIP Use a dry brush to base coat the soap; water will keep the paint from sticking.

Store-bought cards don't compare to handmade greeting cards, and these aren't just handmade, they're fingerprinted! We've created a family of reindeer faces; you can use your fingerprints to make any real or imagined creature that tickles your fancy.

20 pieces card stock (white, ivory, or parchment) or ready-made blank greeting cards

Scissors

Brown stamp pads (for reindeer faces)

Colored markers

Individual letter stamps or a Season's Greetings stamp

Pencil with new eraser tip

Red, blue, or green stamp pads (for embellishments)

Cut your card stock to the desired size. These cards look great postcard style (3 x 5 inches) or cut 6 x 5 and folded in the middle.

Use a thumb or fingerprint to create each reindeer face. Press firmly and evenly onto the stamp pad. Quickly and carefully press your stamped thumb or finger onto the front of your card to make a print. Your thumbprint will make a larger face (daddy reindeer, perhaps?), while your pinky will make the smallest face (baby reindeer). If you are making a reindeer family, space each thumb or fingerprint about ½ inch apart and center them as best you can on the front of your card.

Draw 2 black dots for eyes in the center of each fingerprint. Take a red marker and make a small circle for the nose and fill it in. With a brown marker, make 2 antlers on top of each reindeer head.

Underneath the faces, use your individual stamps to spell out a message like "Peace" or "Love" or use a "Season's Greetings" stamp.

With the tip of an eraser, stamp colored dots carefully along one or all of the edges to create a border, completing your handmade masterpiece. Let dry thoroughly.

MAKES 20 CARDS

TIP Practice making clear fingerprints on a scrap piece of paper before making your card.

WINTER WONDERLAND
Holiday Centerpiece

This centerpiece will make your table complete for the holidays. It conjures up all our fantasies of a winter wonderland … charming houses, a colorful old-fashioned train, and puffy, adorable snowmen—a few of whom are skiing their way through the sparkling dusting of snow. Note that you will need to purchase the railway cake pan at a Williams-Sonoma store to create this. We like their vanilla cake for this as well.

Railway cake pan (15½ x 9¾ x 1¾ inches; see craft introduction)

2 x 2-foot square white foam core

3 cups Royal Icing (page 59)

Black licorice laces

1 or 2 (12-ounce) bags sweetened shredded coconut

Clear rock candy, broken into pieces

Powdered sugar or icing, for the cakes

RAILWAY CAKES

1⅛ cups all-purpose flour

¾ cup plus 2 tablespoons granulated sugar

1 teaspoon baking powder

½ teaspoon baking soda

½ teaspoon kosher salt

4 ounces (1 stick) unsalted butter, melted

½ cup sour cream

2 large eggs

1½ teaspoons vanilla extract

GRAHAM CRACKER HOUSES

1½ cups prepared white frosting

2 teaspoons cream of tartar

27 squares graham crackers

18 mini Oreo sandwich cookies or Necco wafers

Candies (Life Savers, peppermints, etc.)

5 to 10 recipes Frosty and Friends: Marshmallow Snowman (page 51)

 To make the cakes: Have all the ingredients at room temperature.

 Position a rack in the lower third of the oven and preheat it to 350 degrees F. Grease and flour the wells of the railway cake pan and dust with flour.

 Sift the flour, granulated sugar, baking powder, baking soda, and salt into the bowl of an electric mixer.

In a separate bowl, whisk together the melted butter, sour cream, eggs, and vanilla until combined. Fit the mixer with the flat beater. Add the butter mixture to the flour mixture and beat on the lowest speed until the dry ingredients are moistened, 15 to 20 seconds. Stop the mixer and scrape down the sides of the bowl. Increase the speed to medium and beat for 30 seconds.

continued ···>

🍬 **Spoon the batter** evenly into the prepared wells. Tap the pan firmly on the countertop to release any air bubbles. To ensure good details on the cakes, spread the batter so it reaches the top edges of each well and is slightly lower in the center of the well. Bake until a toothpick inserted into the center of a cake comes out clean, 18 to 22 minutes.

🍬 **Transfer the pan** to a wire rack and let cool for 10 minutes, then invert the cakes onto the rack and let cool for at least 1 hour before decorating.

🍬 **Dust the cooled cakes** with powdered sugar or decorate with your favorite frosting and candies.

🍬 **To make the houses:** In a small bowl, combine the frosting and cream of tartar; set aside. This will be your mortar for building the houses.

🍬 **Use 1 graham cracker for the floor** and 4 for the walls. Seal all the seams with the frosting mixture. Using a serrated knife, carefully cut a graham cracker diagonally, creating two triangle shapes; attach them to opposite ends of the house to form roof supports. Attach the sides of 2 graham cracker halves to the top of the house to create a roof. Let the frosting dry for at least 30 minutes. Make 2 more houses this way.

🍬 **Cut the remaining graham crackers** to use for windows and doors, sealing them to the houses with the frosting. Separate the mini Oreos or wafers to create round tiles for the roof, and make sure to attach them with the frosting. Decorate the house with candies, frosting, etc. Let the houses dry for at least 30 minutes before handling them.

🍬 **To make the centerpiece:** Spread the top surface of your foam core with the Royal Icing. This will act as glue. Use the licorice laces to make "train tracks." Attach your train, houses, and snowmen to make a scene. Sprinkle the icing with shredded coconut and broken pieces of rock candy to create a snowy, icy look, and violà! You have a winter wonderland!

MAKES 1 CENTERPIECE

✻ JINGLING JEWEL BALLS
Beaded Pipe Cleaner Ornaments

Kids will love to make their very own ornaments to decorate the Christmas tree. Whether shiny, colorful, eclectic, or stylized, each ornament can be a true extension of the maker's personality. Bring a bag of sparkly gold or silver pipe cleaners and beads to a tree-trimming party, and give friends, cousins, aunts, and uncles a chance to bead to their hearts' delight!

30 colorful pipe cleaners

Large assortment of beads (5 to 10 millimeter diameter)

Scissors

✻ **Take 2 pipe cleaners** and form an X. Twist the X in the center so that it is secure, and then attach 1 or 2 more pipe cleaners by twisting them in the center so that there are 6 or 8 "legs" coming out from the center. Make sure they are securely twisted.

✻ **Bend each pipe cleaner upward,** beginning to form a ball shape.

✻ **Thread your beads** onto each leg, leaving about an inch of room at the tips. (For a more airy look, leave a little more room between each bead.) Secure tips by twisting them together, completing the ball shape of the ornament.

✻ **Cut about 2 inches** from a new pipe cleaner, and twist half of it in the center of the ball to secure, and with the remaining inch, create a hook on the top of the ornament.

MAKES 6 ORNAMENTS

STELLAR STOCKINGS
Handmade Stockings

Stuffed with a batch of homemade cookies or candies, these easy-to-make stockings are great gifts for teachers, babysitters, or your family doctor. Or, glue on a felt nose, mouth, eyes, whiskers, and a pair of floppy dog ears or pointy cat ears, and make it for your pet! Wouldn't Fluffy be pleased with a new rhinestone collar and some catnip?

Felt (in various colors)
Broad-tipped marker
Straight pins or masking tape
Fabric scissors
Hot-glue gun

Embroidery floss
Wide-eyed needle
Buttons and beads, for decorating
Ribbon

Draw a stocking shape on a piece of felt with your marker. Before cutting, place another piece of felt underneath the first piece. Line them up and pin or tape them together so that when you cut out the stocking shape, both pieces of felt end up looking the same. Cut just inside the line where you've drawn the pattern, so that marker isn't visible on your felt cutout.

On one of the felt cutouts, apply a line of hot glue ¼ inch from the edge along both sides and around the foot, but not across the top. Place the second cutout on top of the first, so that the edges match up. Place a heavy book on top of them to make the seams stick (approximately 5 minutes). Once the glue is dry, use embroidery floss and a wide-eyed needle to accent the seam with decorative stitching.

Personalize it! If the stocking is for a math teacher, for example, glue on some cutout felt numbers. For a grandma who likes to sew, glue on colorful buttons. For friends, cut out felt initials and stud them with shiny beads. So many options!

Make a hanger for the stocking by looping in a piece of ribbon and stitching the knot to the back of the felt.

MAKES SEVERAL STOCKINGS

JOLLY COOKIE JAR
Cookie Fixings Layered in a Jar with Recipe

This one-of-a-kind, do-it-yourself layered glass cookie jar comes with all the necessary dry ingredients already measured out! It's a "just add butter, eggs, and vanilla" kind of gift, which will delight grown-ups and kids alike. Any favorite cookie recipe will do, however we chose a recipe with walnuts, dried cherries, and chocolate chips for a festive look and delicious taste!

1-quart wide-mouthed jar (with a lid) in glass or clear plastic
¼ cup granulated sugar
¾ cup packed light brown sugar
¾ cup all-purpose flour
¼ teaspoon baking soda

¼ teaspoon baking powder
½ cup chopped walnuts
½ cup dried tart cherries
½ cup rolled oats (not instant)
¾ cup semisweet chocolate chips
3 x 3-inch piece white card stock

Hole punch
16 to 18 inches narrow ribbon or kitchen string

☃ **Add each ingredient** into the jar in the order listed. After each addition, use a large spoon or a small fist to level and pack down each layer. Attach the lid.

☃ **On the white card stock,** make a gift tag that includes the following instructions: "For scrumptious holiday cookies in a flash, preheat the oven to 375 degrees F. Beat together 3 ounces (¾ stick) softened unsalted butter, ½ teaspoon vanilla extract, and 1 egg in a large bowl or mixer. Add the contents of the jar and stir or mix until well blended. Drop by rounded spoonfuls onto an ungreased cookie sheet. Bake until golden, 7 to 10 minutes. Makes 2 dozen cookies. Enjoy!"

☃ **Punch a hole in a corner of your gift tag,** and thread your ribbon or kitchen string through. When the tag is centered in the middle of the ribbon, tie the ribbon around the jar's neck, or secure it under the threads of the lid.

MAKES 1 JAR

SPARKLING SUPERSTAR
3-D Curled Paper Star

Made with gold or silver wrapping paper, this amazing star makes an incredible party decoration. Make several and hang them at varied lengths from a ceiling and the entire room will be transformed!

Ruler
Pencil
Scissors

Thick gold or silver wrapping paper
Clear tape

Hole punch
Kitchen string

❄ **Measure, mark, and cut** eight 5 x 5-inch squares from the wrapping paper. These will form the 8 sections (or arms) of your star.

❄ **Fold 1 of the squares in half** on the diagonal to form a triangle (shiny side out). Fold your paper in half again to make a smaller triangle. Fold the short point of the triangle (where the two equal sides connect) to the center of the long side of the triangle (its base) to make a trapezoid shape. Fold in half again in the same direction. Now your folded shape will look like a flattened cylinder with points (a compressed trapezoid).

❄ **Unfold 2 times** (back to your small triangle shape). Carefully cut along the 3 crease lines, starting at the open edge and each time stopping ½ inch before the folded edge. Now unfold your paper back to its original square shape, shiny side up.

❄ **Roll up the first 2 innermost points** of the cutout to form a small ring. Slightly overlap and tape the two points together. Flip the cutout over, bring up the next 2 inner points and tape together. Repeat two more times so that all of the paper lines have been joined, including the outer points. You have now completed one of the 8 sections of your star. Repeat with the remaining squares of paper to make 7 more "arms."

❄ **Lay the 8 arms in a row**, with the outer ring of one touching the middle ring (the third set of points you taped) of the next and so forth. Tape each of the 8 arms together, middle ring of one to outer ring of the next, to form a chain. Finally, tape the first and last arms together to form the star!

❄ **Secure it!** Tape the tips together in the center of your star. Punch a hole near the top of any of the points, and gently loop a string through to hang.

MAKES 1 STAR

PUFFY PALS
Pom-Pom Animals in a Decorative Box

These sweet, little friends can be pasted into their special little box homes, and hung on a Christmas tree, pasted on a card, or just played with. Create any variation on a puffy pal.

Newspaper

Hot-glue gun

6 small, decorative craft boxes, lids removed (lids aren't necessary for this project)

6 large pom-poms in any color (body)

6 medium pom-poms in any color (head)

12 small wiggle eyes

12 small pom-poms in any color (ears)

2 feet silk ribbon (any color), cut into 4-inch lengths

Cover a work surface with newspaper. Lay your materials out on the newspaper.

Heat your glue gun for 5 minutes (have a grown-up help you).

Place a dot of glue inside the bottom of a box. Press a large pom-pom into the box for 10 seconds.

Put a dot of glue on the large pom-pom where you want to place the head. Press a medium pom-pom on the spot with the glue; hold for 10 seconds.

Put 2 spots of glue on either side of the medium pom-pom; press on 2 eyes and hold for 10 seconds each. After the eyes are attached, attach the ears. Put 2 spots of glue on the medium pom-pom, and press 2 small pom-poms into place for about 10 seconds each.

Decide which part of the box will be upright when hanging, and dot it there with glue. Loop a piece of ribbon and attach it to the glue; hold for 10 seconds. Let the finished ornament set for about 5 minutes. Your ornament is now ready for hanging.

Repeat with the other materials to make 5 more Puffy Pals.

MAKES 6 ORNAMENTS

GRINCH'S GROOVY GIFT TIN
Candy Cane–Decorated Tin Pail

Not only is this candy cane–covered tin pail great for filling with Sugarplum Lollies (page 36) or Celebration Sticks (page 42) and giving as a gift, but filled with fresh flowers, it also makes a fantastic centerpiece for a holiday table. We've used galvanized metal tins, painted tins, and even a clean 32-ounce soup or tomato can for this.

Enough candy canes to wrap around your tin

Hot-glue gun

Galvanized tin pail (plain or painted) or soup can that is no taller than the candy canes you use

Clear nail polish

2 feet ribbon (optional)

Figure out how many candy canes you will need to encircle your pail and unwrap them.

With a glue gun, carefully glue a line down the back of each candy cane, and attach it vertically to the outside wall of the pail, so that the candy cane's loop is facing outward at the top of the pail. Each candy cane should be about ⅛ inch apart. These candy canes are no longer edible!!!

To add a beautiful gloss, and to prevent the candy canes from becoming sticky, carefully brush a coat or two of clear nail polish on them.

You can now tie a ribbon around the center or top third of the pail if you like. Dot hot glue around the circumference and attach the ribbon.

MAKES 1 GIFT TIN

LET THERE BE LIGHT
Colorful Beeswax Candle

A wonderful holiday tradition to start with kids, this beautiful, clean-burning candle lights up the night. Make a variety, using shades of red and/or green beeswax sheets for Christmas candles, blue and white for Hanukkah, or red, black, and green for Kwanzaa. Or, just mix a palette of unique colors and create a rainbow of gorgeous light!

Beeswax sheet in color of your choice, cut to size (see Tip)
Large sheet butcher paper

Primed wick
Scissors (for cutting wick)

❄ **Unroll the beeswax sheet** on a work surface covered with butcher paper (newspaper may bleed onto light-colored beeswax).

❄ **Cut your wick,** making sure it is about 2 inches longer than the height of your beeswax sheet.

❄ **Place the wick along the edge** of the beeswax sheet, and fold the sheet approximately ⅛ inch over the wick. Press down gently on the sheet to make sure the wax completely surrounds the wick. (You can use a hair dryer for 10 to 15 seconds to warm the wax and secure the wick.)

❄ **Once the wick is firmly secured** in the beeswax sheet, begin to roll. Roll the candle slowly, and be sure to keep the edges aligned.

❄ **After reaching the end of the sheet,** gently press down on the exposed edge to make sure that your candle does not come apart. (Here again, you can use a hair dryer to warm the exposed edge before you press down.)

❄ **Decide which end will be the top** of the candle, and trim the wick down to approximately ½ inch. Cut the exposed wick completely from the bottom end. Glow on!

MAKES 1 CANDLE

TIP We suggest a beeswax sheet 6 to 8 inches long, by at least 8 inches wide. These can be purchased at craft stores or online.

SWEET AND CRUNCHY GARLAND
Popcorn, Gumdrop, and Candy Garland

There are many kinds of garland, but the best is the kind you can eat! We love to do this as a group activity, with the whole family creating their own delicious, pretty garland.

Wide-eyed needle
Fishing line or thread

15 cups (popped) popcorn
6 cups gumdrops

3 cups colorful Life Savers

❋ **Decide on the length** of garland you intend to make (the materials listed here will yield a 10-foot garland). Thread the needle with that length of fishing line or thread.

❋ **Tie a large double knot** at the end of the line. Put the needle through as many popcorn kernels as you would like, then move on to the gumdrops or Life Savers, threading them through the middle.

❋ **Keep threading the various items** until you're nearly done, remembering to leave room to tie off the garland. You can nibble at this garland for the first 3 days; after that it's purely decorative. (When the holiday season is over, you should throw it away.)

❋ **It's fun to come up with patterns** you'd like to repeat, such as 5 popcorns, 3 red Life Savers, 2 green gumdrops, 2 white gumdrops. Repeat.

MAKES ONE 10-FOOT GARLAND

TIP Use a dampened paper towel to clean the needle in between threading items.

FUNKY FLEECE HAT
Handmade Hat

Cozy fleece hats are perfect for wearing (and sharing) during the cold holiday season. These easy-to-make head warmers will keep you both stylish and warm!

Tape measure

½ yard fleece fabric

Good scissors (for cutting fabric)

Needle and thread

Felt cutout or large button

1 yard cloth ribbon or colored cord

Using a tape measure, measure the circumference of the head to be covered. Add 2 inches to this measurement. This will be your final measurement.

Cut a piece of fleece that's 18 inches wide and as long as your final measurement.

Fold the fleece in half, right side in, so that the wide 18-inch edges match up. Sew a ½-inch-wide seam along the first 13 inches of this edge. You will have 5 inches left unsewn. Just below your last stitch, make a ½-inch cut in from the side. Turn your hat rightside out, and sew a ½-inch seam along the last 5 inches of unsewn fleece so the seam doesn't show when this bottom of the hat is rolled to form the cuff.

Roll the bottom of your hat up twice. This will be the cuff. Sew a felt cutout or large button onto this cuff to prevent it from unrolling.

Finish it! Gather the top 4 or 5 inches of the hat and tie a cloth ribbon or colorful cord around it in a stylish bow or funky knot. You can accentuate the gathering at the top by cutting the fleece in 1- to 2-inch lengthwise strips and tying a small knot at the end of each strip or letting them flop over.

MAKES 1 HAT

TIP Optionally, sew buttons to the ends of the tied on cloth ribbon for added embellishment

INDEX

TABLE OF EQUIVALENTS

The exact equivalents in the following table have been rounded for convenience.

LIQUID/DRY MEASURES

U.S.	Metric
¼ teaspoon	1.25 milliliters
½ teaspoon	2.5 milliliters
1 teaspoon	5 milliliters
1 tablespoon (3 teaspoons)	15 milliliters
1 fluid ounce (2 tablespoons)	30 milliliters
¼ cup	60 milliliters
⅓ cup	80 milliliters
½ cup	120 milliliters
1 cup	240 milliliters
1 pint (2 cups)	480 milliliters
1 quart (4 cups; 32 ounces)	960 milliliters
1 gallon (4 quarts)	3.84 liters
1 ounce (by weight)	28 grams
1 pound	454 grams
2.2 pounds	1 kilogram

LENGTHS

U.S.	Metric
⅛ inch	3 millimeters
¼ inch	6 millimeters
½ inch	12 millimeters
1 inch	2.5 centimeters

OVEN TEMPERATURES

Fahrenheit	Celsius	Gas
250	120	½
275	140	1
300	150	2
325	160	3
350	180	4
375	190	5
400	200	6
425	220	7
450	230	8
475	240	9
500	260	10